TRAINS *of* DISCOVERY

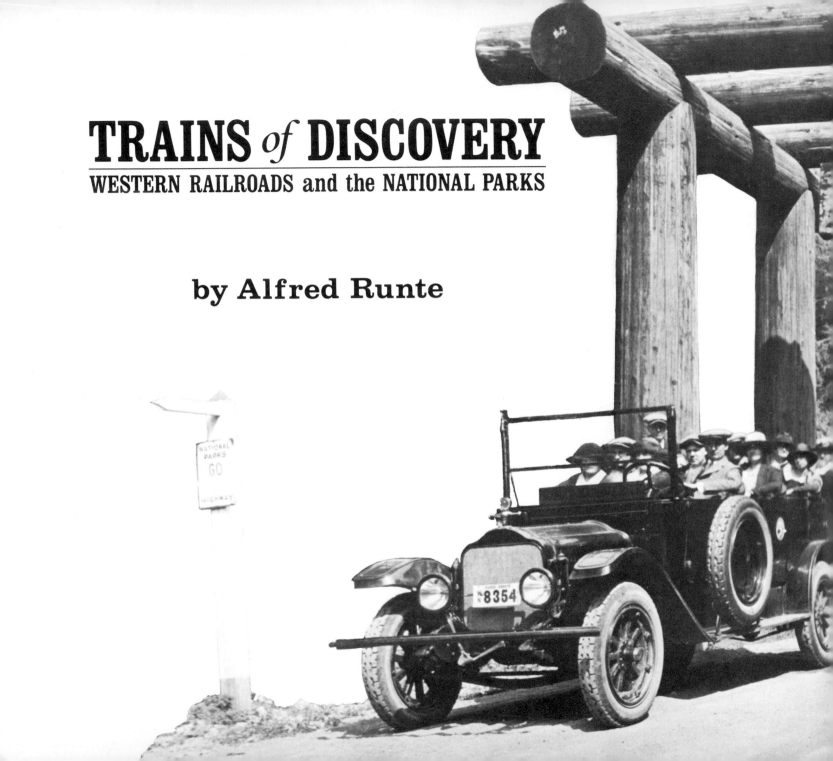

TRAINS *of* DISCOVERY
WESTERN RAILROADS and the NATIONAL PARKS

by Alfred Runte

MT. RAINIER NATIONAL PARK

NORTHLAND PRESS ✦ FLAGSTAFF, ARIZONA

For Carl Bajema, David Corbin, Bill Johnson, Arthur Lloyd,
Walter Smith, and Dan Monaghan, special friends who have shared with me the beauty of the West
and the call of the rails; and for
Richard M. Bressler, who made the history live again.

Half title vignette: " 'North Coast Limited' at Livingston, Montana" photo-illustration of the Northern Pacific's premier passenger train, from Wonderland, 1904. Courtesy of the Pacific Northwest Collection, University of Washington Libraries, Seattle.

Frontispiece: Motor stages pass under the entrance arch to Mount Rainier National Park, ca. 1925. Courtesy of Burlington Northern Inc.

CONTENTS

"All aboard on the Empire Builder . . . *," photograph from* Glacier Park in Pictures, *a Great Northern Railway brochure, ca. 1940. Courtesy of the Pacific Northwest Collection, University of Washington Libraries, Seattle.*

ACKNOWLEDGMENTS

THE COMPLETION of this project owes much to the cooperation of friends, librarians, archivists, and corporate officials. I am especially indebted to Bill Johnson of Jay Rockey Public Relations, Seattle, Washington, for teaching me so many things about art reproduction, photography, and commercial design. Mary Vocelka, research librarian with the National Park Service in Yosemite, and her assistant, Linda Eade, made one discovery after another on my behalf. Tom DuRant, librarian of the Branch of Graphics Research, National Park Service, Springfield, Virginia, also shared the gems of his collection, many previously unpublished. Walter P. Gray III, archivist at the California State Railroad Museum, and Tere Silva of the California State Library, both in Sacramento, generously opened their collections as well.

My gratitude to Richard M. Bressler, chairman and chief executive officer of Burlington Northern Inc., is noted in the introduction. Allan R. Boyce and Wayne W. Hopkins of Burlington Northern Inc., Public Affairs division also read portions of the manuscript and offered suggestions. I am equally grateful for the assistance of the Santa Fe Railway Company, whose curators, W. D. Woodburn and Paul D. Benisek, opened the Collection of Southwestern Art for my inspection and use. John E. Witherbee, research specialist for the Union Pacific Railroad Company, forwarded photographs, menu covers, and brochures for examination and reproduction. Donald Peterson and Lyn Topinka of the United States Geological Survey, Vancouver, Washington, lent photographs tracing the eruption of Mount St. Helens.

At the University of Washington, Glenda Pearson

This 1904 Wonderland *photo-illustration depicts
from top to bottom: "Northern Pacific Railway
Observation Car . . . Day Coach . . . Dining Car . . .
Standard Pullman Sleeping Car." Courtesy of
the Pacific Northwest Collection, University of
Washington Libraries, Seattle.*

and Susan Cunningham rummaged through the stacks of the Pacific Northwest Collection for early railroad guidebooks, pamphlets, and memorabilia; Stan Shockey and Nancy Hines of Instructional Media Services meticulously photographed each work of art I selected. I am also grateful for the photographic assistance of Shirley Burman in Sacramento, California, and Michael Dixon and Brian Grogan in Yosemite National Park. Frank Conlon, Frank Freidel, Robert E. Burke, and W. J. Rorabaugh, my colleagues in the Department of History, critically read all or portions of the manuscript. Carol Zabilski of the Office of Scholarly Journals provided helpful editorial advice.

Finally, I am indebted to the National Parks and Conservation Association and Burlington Northern Inc., for permission to rewrite and republish portions of my work which originally appeared as follows: "Pragmatic Alliance: Western Railroads and the National Parks," *National Parks and Conservation Magazine: The Environmental Journal* 48 (April 1974):14–21; "Yosemite Valley Railroad: Highway of History, Pathway of Promise," *National Parks and Conservation Magazine. The Environmental Journal* 48 (December 1974):4–9; and *Burlington Northern and the Dedication of Mount St. Helens: New Legacy of a Proud Tradition* (Seattle: Burlington Northern Inc., 1982).

An observation car of the Yosemite Valley Railroad, ca. 1908, when passenger trains, like women's hats, were in fashion. Courtesy of the National Park Service, Yosemite Collections.

INTRODUCTION

THE UNITED STATES, recognized for its Declaration of Independence and the Constitution, has also bequeathed to the world its most stunning example of landscape democracy—the national park idea. Yet, few people realize how much this idea owes to not only John Muir, members of the Sierra Club, and other like-minded idealists, but to a major corporate group, the railroads of the American West. Like most, I was largely unaware of the commitment among western railroads to promote the national parks—that is, until 1973, when the first energy crisis in the United States reawakened the public's consciousness regarding the need to find alternative forms of transportation to replace the automobile. At the time, I was pursuing research for my book, *National Parks: The American Experience* (1979), a history of the national park idea. The more I examined the social, cultural, and intellectual origins of the national park system, the more I discovered the great debt owed to the railroads of the West for both endorsing and developing the national parks during those early, difficult years.

Initially, in a series of articles, I explored the historical relationship between the railroads and the national parks. Later, I prepared a slide lecture on the topic, relying on advertisements and photographs from various eras. I never expected the enthusiasm these talks sparked among my audiences, especially senior citizens' groups, for whom the slides and narrative evoked fond memories of riding the western rails in years gone by.

During the summer of 1980, when I first joined the National Park Service as a seasonal interpreter in Yosemite Valley, I realized that such a lecture would be a "natural" for my weekly series of evening programs. Indeed, the response from park visitors was overwhelming. I would frequently spend an hour after each program meeting with visitors who wanted to reminisce about traveling through the West by rail. Inevitably, the question was asked:

Every summer between 1915 and 1927 the Great Northern Railway added open observation cars to its transcontinental trains to provide unobstructed views of Glacier National Park. Courtesy of Burlington Northern Inc.

6

"Where can I read more about the material you presented this evening?" Unfortunately, I could only direct these individuals to my previously published articles, now well-sandwiched away on the shelves of distant libraries.

As a result, following my second season in Yosemite Valley, I decided to draw these publications together, rewrite them to reflect my subsequent research, and publish them as an illustrated monograph suitable for distribution and sale in national park bookstores. But again, I was unable to appreciate fully where my interest in the topic was heading. That fall, when I returned to my position in the history department of the University of Washington in Seattle, Richard Bressler, chairman and chief executive officer of Burlington Northern Inc., asked me to prepare an article suitable for the company's proposed gift of a tract of land on Mount St. Helens to the federal government. With that request, I realized that there still survived a glimmer of the history I had been extolling for a decade; I am therefore very pleased that this volume concludes with a discussion of Burlington Northern's donation of that land parcel to the federal government, thus restoring the whole of Mount St. Helens to the American people.

The inspiration for this book was that once-flourishing "pragmatic alliance" between America's railroads and the national parks. Much of that history has been forgotten since the automobile came to dominate the national transportation scene. Fortunately, the knowledgeable traveler can still recapture this legacy at both Denali (Mount McKinley) National Park in Alaska, and Glacier National Park in northwestern Montana. The former, served by the Alaska Railroad, offers wilderness enthusiasts the chance to experience what the national parks were like at the turn of the century, when all were far removed from the boundaries of civilization. Similarly, Glacier National Park, on the main line of Amtrak's *Empire Builder,* preserves that golden age of passenger railroading in the United States, a time during which not only Glacier but Yellowstone, Yosemite, and the Grand Canyon were directly accessible by passenger trains.

My intent is not to look backward for its own sake, but to remind Americans of the price our nation has paid, both socially and environmentally, for its unqualified love affair with the automobile. If the national parks are to survive the pavement, congestion, and pollution that the automobile leaves in its wake, a better way of transporting visitors must be found. Only public transportation—required for everyone, excluding no one—promises to serve both the needs of access *and* preservation. It is in this spirit that I invite everyone to heed the familiar cry "All aboard!" and join me as our streamliner of history glides westward once again toward America's wonderlands—the national parks.

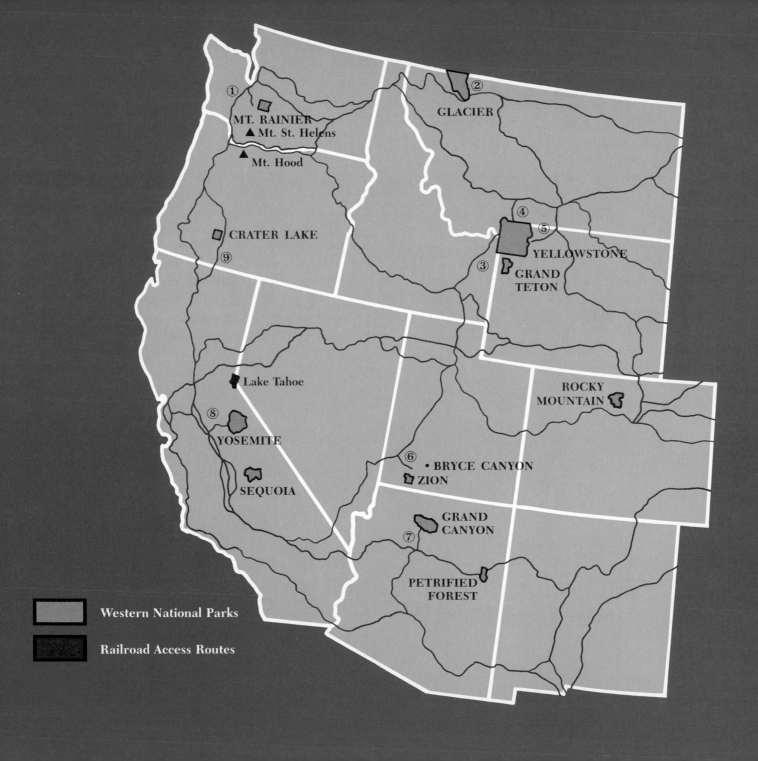

① MT. RAINIER

▲ Mt. St. Helens

▲ Mt. Hood

② GLACIER

CRATER LAKE
⑨

④
⑤
YELLOWSTONE
③
GRAND
TETON

Lake Tahoe

ROCKY
MOUNTAIN

⑧
YOSEMITE

⑥ • BRYCE CANYON
ZION

SEQUOIA

⑦ GRAND
CANYON

PETRIFIED
FOREST

Western National Parks

Railroad Access Routes

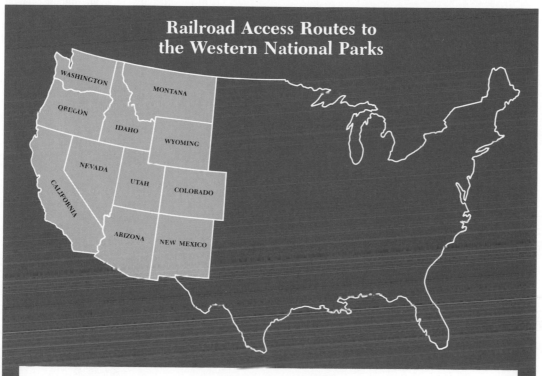

Railroad Access Routes to the Western National Parks

Railroad Lines

① Great Northern, Union Pacific, Northern Pacific railroads
② Great Northern Railway, mainline connections to Glacier National Park
③ Yellowstone Branch, Union Pacific Railroad
④ Yellowstone Branch, Northern Pacific Railroad
⑤ Cody Branch (Yellowstone gateway); Chicago, Burlington & Quincy Railroad
⑥ Cedar City Branch (Zion, Bryce, North Rim Grand Canyon gateway), Union Pacific Railroad
⑦ Grand Canyon Branch; Atchison, Topeka & Santa Fe Railway
⑧ Yosemite Valley Railroad
⑨ Southern Pacific Railroad

Hectic scenes, such as this ca. 1916 view of the platform of the El Portal Station, gateway to Yosemite, at train time demonstrate the public's reliance on the western railroads for transportation to the national parks. Passengers arriving on the Yosemite Valley Railroad boarded waiting motor stages for the remaining one hour and thirty-five minute trip to hotels in Yosemite Valley. Courtesy of the National Park Service, Yosemite Collections.

PROLOGUE
The Romantic Terminus

The western margin of this continent is built of a succession of mountain chains folded in broad corrugations, like waves of stone upon whose seaward base beat the mild small breakers of the Pacific. By far the grandest of these ranges is the Sierra Nevada, . . . its crest a line of sharp, snowy peaks springing into the sky and catching the alpenglow *long after the sun has set for all the rest of America.*

Clarence King, 1871

ANYONE who has thumbed through the pages of an old newspaper or magazine, or gazed intently into the faded reality of a long-forgotten photograph, may recall the sensation of being "lost," if only momentarily, in the era depicted. What follows is a similar attempt to recapture the spirit of a particular age in all its visual drama and literary exuberance. The subject is railroads—their destination, the national parks. Singled out for emphasis is the eighty-year period between 1880 and 1960, during which Americans were either dependent on rail transportation or still accustomed to considering passenger trains as a serious option for pleasure travel.

In this volume, the reader will find original pieces of railroad art or advertising copy, carefully reproduced to reflect the elegance of their initial unveiling. Similarly, the photographs have been chosen to suggest the excitement of visiting the national parks during that age when the word "West" was still synonymous with high adventure.

Well into the twentieth century, as the artistic and literary achievements of the Romantic Movement were still fresh in the minds of Americans, the railroads of the West enjoyed a marketing advantage that was second to none. Theirs was the "romantic terminus." Americans have been drawn to the West

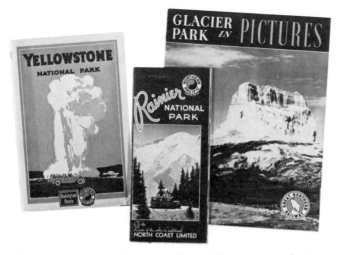

Original railroad guidebook and pamphlet covers. Left: *Courtesy of the author.* Center: *Courtesy of the Pacific Northwest Collection, University of Washington Libraries, Seattle.* Right: *Courtesy of Burlington Northern Inc.*

not only by its history but also by its topography. Westward expansion provided Americans with the opportunity to play out their final act of territorial development against such imposing backdrops as Yellowstone, Mount Rainier, the Grand Canyon, and the Yosemite Valley. These very western landscapes inspired the first national parks: ecology was not the nation's concern at the turn of the century, but rather, the preservation of these last vestiges of the unspoiled "romantic horizon" was at stake.

Among all the publicists of the region, the railroads were without rivals in their ability to bring the West into the living rooms of the American people with special attention given to its cultural and topographical significance. The development of the national parks coincided perfectly with the lines' marketing strategy. Economically speaking, the enticement of settlers and city-builders from the security of the East to the uncertainties of the new frontier demanded the stimulation that only the power of suggestion could provide. Standard advertising copy wrapped the West in an array of superlatives, giving special attention to its unlimited potential for economic growth, built on a vast foundation of national resources. Underground minerals and fields not yet broken to the plow were hard to visualize, however; potential was not reality. In the meantime, people needed some tangible evidence of abundance. Thus, by creatively drawing attention to the scale of western topography, the railroads discovered one subtle means of suggesting to prospective migrants that, as claimed, the region must indeed be equally well-endowed with hidden wealth.

Rail travel was, in this respect, a means to a greater end; those who were tourists one day might in fact decide to become settlers the next. In another sense, tourism was also a lucrative end in itself. For decades, Americans in search of spectacular scenery had traveled almost exclusively to such eastern wonders as the Natural Bridge in Virginia, the Hudson River highlands, and Niagara Falls in New York.

Left: *The Great Northern Railway combined mountain grandeur, Blackfoot Indian culture, and luxurious accommodations in this 1915 advertisement featuring Glacier National Park. Reprinted by permission of Burlington Northern Inc.*

With the completion of the first transcontinental railroad in 1869, these wealthy patrons of America's great eastern resorts could realistically think about seeing the West as well.

For the next half century, the railroads of the region did everything possible to stimulate that interest. Partly a quest for profits, partly a means of achieving greater recognition and prestige, the campaign elevated railroad executives to positions of importance and influence as patrons of the arts. As early as 1903, for example, the Santa Fe Railway began acquiring paintings about the Grand Canyon, the Petrified Forest, and other southwestern subjects for its stations and executive suites. Similarly, in 1898 the Southern Pacific Railroad founded *Sunset,* a monthly magazine supporting scores of creative individuals, especially artists, photographers, and journalists.

Whatever the medium or the occasion, national parks were primary attractions for promotional efforts. As masterpieces of nature, the parks set the standard for artworks that the railroads hoped would attract both settlers and tourists to the romantic West. Today, awareness of ecological needs has diffused much of that initial innocence, spontaneity, and enthusiasm for national park promotion. Nevertheless, the color and elegance of the period are timeless.

With the growing availability of color printing at the turn of the century, railroad promotion of the West and the national parks entered a new and exciting era. Above: A 1915 Northern Pacific brochure cover, "Pacific Coast Attractions," highlights the beauty, comfort, and convenience of the Yellowstone Park line. Courtesy of the California State Railroad Museum, Sacramento.

Left: A 1929 advertisement extolls the thrill of discovering the North Rim of the Grand Canyon. Reprinted by permission of the Union Pacific Railroad Company. Above: ". . . In All Its Glory" shows the rugged beauty of the Rocky Mountains in 1948 from a vista dome car. Reprinted by permission of the Budd Company.

TRAINS *of* DISCOVERY

· C H A P T E R ·

1

Several women at Yellowstone's
Old Faithful Inn in 1922, after a tour in a
Park Service car. Considered a novelty barely a decade earlier, the automobile
had invaded the national parks in record numbers by the 1920s. Yellowstone
National Park photograph (3295). Courtesy of the National Park Service.

Thomas Moran's oil painting, The Grand Canyon of the Yellowstone, *was completed in the spring of 1872. Watercolors and sketches by the artist helped inspire the U.S. Congress to pass legislation leading to the creation of Yellowstone National Park, Wyoming, on March 1, 1872. Courtesy of the National Museum of American Art, Smithsonian Institution, Washington, D.C. Lent by U.S. Department of the Interior, National Park Service.*

THE NORTHERN PACIFIC RAILROAD
Yellowstone Park Line

The traveler who has journeyed eastward to climb the castled crags of Rhineland and survey the mighty peaks and wondrous glaciers of the Alps, who has . . . gazed upon the marvelous creations of Michelangelo and Da Vinci; and stood within the shadow of the pyramids,—may well turn westward to view the greater wonders of his own land.

Beyond the Great Lakes, far from the hum of New England factories, far from the busy throngs of Broadway, from the smoke and grime of iron cities, and the dull, prosaic life of many another Eastern town, lies a region which may justly be designated the Wonderland of the World.

Charles S. Fee, General Passenger Agent, Northern Pacific Railroad, 1885

AMONG THE METHODS of conservation in the United States, the national park idea has been heralded as America's purest expression of landscape democracy. As a result, the mere suggestion that an institution so famous for its idealism and philanthropy would receive a crucial boost from industry may seem almost sacrilegious. According to popular tradition, the explorers who opened Yellowstone in 1870 conceived the national park idea while unraveling the mysteries of the region. But at best, ecology and altruism were afterthoughts of the Yellowstone Park campaign. From the outset, establishment of the park owed far more to the financier Jay

Cooke and to officials of the Northern Pacific Railroad—all of whom, upon completion of the line, expected to profit from the territory as a great tourist resort.

As the more patriotic and unselfish account, the popular depiction of the origins of Yellowstone National Park has obviously been less difficult to embrace. According to this version, the national park idea was not born in a corporate boardroom; instead, it came into being on the night of September 19, 1870, when members of the celebrated Washburn Expedition settled down around their campfire to share impressions of the wonderland that they had just finished exploring. Apparently, one of the men proposed that each member of the party claim a tract of land surrounding the canyon or the geyser basins for personal gain. Cornelius Hedges, a young lawyer from Helena, Montana, strongly disagreed, and pleaded with the explorers to abandon any private ambitions in the interest of promoting Yellowstone as a great national park for all Americans to own and enjoy. Nathaniel Pitt Langford, the noted publicist of the expedition, recorded the following in his diary: "His suggestion met with an instantaneous and favorable response from all—except one—of the members of our party, and each hour since the matter was first broached, our enthusiasm has increased." Thus, Langford concluded his entry for September 20, "I lay awake half of last night thinking about it; and if my wakefulness deprived my bed-fellow (Hedges) of any sleep, he has only himself and his disturbing National Park proposition to answer for it."

There is only one nagging doubt about the accuracy of this statement: Langford did not publish these words until 1905, fully thirty-five years after the event. By then, of course, he and his colleagues had had numerous opportunities to amend their accounts of the expedition in light of the growing fame of the national park idea. Certainly there is something suspicious in the fact that, despite their reported enthusiasm, not one of the eighteen men present around that Yellowstone campfire ever mentioned the national park idea in the articles and speeches prepared immediately afterward. In either case, even if Langford's account were credible, some very important names would still be missing from his story, most notably Jay Cooke, promoter and financier of the Northern Pacific Railroad extension project, and Cooke's office manager, A. B. Nettleton.

Indeed, the explorers' discussion around their campfire that mid-September evening could not have taken place in ignorance of the plans of the Northern Pacific Railroad. Langford must have informed all of the men about Jay Cooke's intentions, including Henry D. Washburn, the surveyor general of Montana and nominal leader of the expedition. Three months prior to the venture, Langford had met personally with Cooke at the latter's estate just outside Philadelphia. Not only did Cooke retain Langford to promote Yellowstone as part of a publicity campaign to secure funding for the railroad, he probably suggested the Washburn Expedition itself. By then, Cooke realized that his right-of-way through south-central Montana would bring him within forty or fifty miles of Yellowstone. Obviously, with such a great wonderland lying along his main line to the Pacific, Cooke stood to become the direct beneficiary of any publicity aimed at introducing the region to prospective travelers.

Meanwhile, following the expedition of 1870, Nathaniel Langford returned east to lecture in New

York, Philadelphia, and Washington, D. C., on behalf of the Northern Pacific. Here again, his writings and statements reveal that he acted more as a promoter rather than as a concerned private citizen speaking only for the protection of Yellowstone. At every opportunity, Langford trumpeted the building of the Northern Pacific Railroad, specifically noting that completion of the line would make Yellowstone "speedily accessible" to tourists.

As a scientist, Professor Ferdinand V. Hayden, a geologist and government surveyor, found Langford's descriptions of Yellowstone's thermal features especially fascinating. Accordingly, he petitioned Congress for extra funding to take his own survey into the region during the summer of 1871. Congress agreed and appropriated $40,000 to ensure that the expedition would be the most complete and systematic ever.

Once more, the office of Jay Cooke intervened in planning for the Hayden Survey on behalf of the Northern Pacific Railroad. Cooke's office manager, A. B. Nettleton, wrote directly to Hayden to request that Thomas Moran, a landscape artist of growing renown, be permitted to accompany the expedition as a private citizen. "Please understand that we do not wish to burden you with more people than you can attend to," Nettleton began his letter, "but I think that Mr. Moran will be a very desirable addition to your expedition. . . ." On a personal note, Nettleton also stressed that the favor would "be a great accommodation" to Jay Cooke and the interests of the railroad. "[Moran], of course, expects to pay his own expenses, and simply wishes to take advantage of your cavalry escort."

In reality, Moran needed financial assistance; like Nathaniel P. Langford, his distant benefactor was none other than Jay Cooke, from whom the artist borrowed the five hundred dollars required to supplement his own meager resources. In this manner, Cooke's endorsement (and funds) directly led to the production of Moran's most famous oil painting, *The Grand Canyon of the Yellowstone*, now housed in the National Museum of American Art, Smithsonian Institution, in Washington, D.C.

As late as September 1871, however, when the Hayden Survey returned from the Yellowstone wilderness, no public campaign to protect the region as a national park had yet been formed. For this reason, the Yellowstone campfire story of 1870 is even more suspect. Certainly, if the explorers of the preceding expedition had pledged themselves to such a grand scheme, they would not have sacrificed another perfect opportunity—in this instance, the publicity generated by the Hayden Survey—to once more introduce the national park idea to the American people. No one came forward, not even Professor Hayden, who had achieved great distinction in the public eye.

Credit for proposing the introduction of legislation to protect Yellowstone as a public park actually rests with officials of the Northern Pacific Railroad project. The clue is to be found in a letter Professor Hayden received on October 28, 1871, from A. B. Nettleton, written on the stationery of Jay Cooke & Co., Bankers, Financial Agents, Northern Pacific Railroad Company. The letter began:

Dear Doctor:
Judge Kelley has made a suggestion which strikes me as being an excellent one, viz: Let Congress pass a bill reserving the Great Geyser Basin as a public park forever—just as it has reserved that far inferior wonder the Yosemite valley and big trees. If you approve this would such a recommendation be appropriate in your official report?

Judge Kelley was Congressman William Darrah Kelley of Philadelphia, a prominent Republican sympathetic to Cooke and his railroad enterprises. Kelley learned about Yellowstone through the published congressional report of Lieutenant Gustavus C. Doane, commander of the cavalry escort for the Washburn Expedition. Nettleton's reference to "Yosemite valley and the big trees" was also significant, for it underscored the crucial matter of precedent. In 1864, Congress had granted Yosemite Valley and the Mariposa Grove of Giant Sequoias to the state of California "for public use, resort, and recreation," to be held "inalienable for all time." Although Yosemite was a state park, its congressional origin was not overlooked by Yellowstone's own champions. Management considerations aside, Nettleton, for one, appreciated that Congress, through the Yosemite grant, had already established a procedure for setting aside unique scenery in the national interest.

Not until Professor Hayden received the letter in question, however, did he or any of the other explorers—including Nathaniel Langford and Cornelius Hedges—actually begin working to have Yellowstone protected as a public park similar to Yosemite. So again, the intervention of the Northern Pacific Railroad, not the latent sympathies of Yellowstone's actual discoverers, was crucial.

From the perspective of the Northern Pacific, the campaign itself was anticlimactic. Having entrusted the idea for a park to Professor Hayden, officials of the railroad stayed out of the limelight on Capitol Hill, confident that Hayden's fame and credibility as a government geologist would guarantee a favorable outcome. They were not to be disappointed, for on March 1, 1872, only three months after being introduced in Congress, the Yellowstone Park Act was signed into law by President Ulysses S. Grant.

Unfortunately for Jay Cooke, his own hopes of opening the Yellowstone country to tourists were

Standing fifty feet high, with a thirty-foot arch, the entrance to Yellowstone National Park, at Gardiner, Montana, welcomed tourists as they got off the Northern Pacific Railroad. From Wonderland, 1904, courtesy of the Pacific Northwest Collection, University of Washington Libraries, Seattle.

23

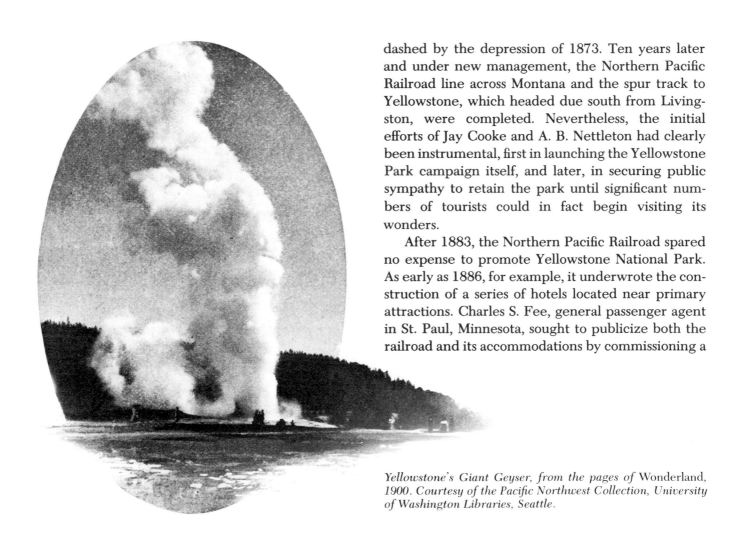

dashed by the depression of 1873. Ten years later and under new management, the Northern Pacific Railroad line across Montana and the spur track to Yellowstone, which headed due south from Livingston, were completed. Nevertheless, the initial efforts of Jay Cooke and A. B. Nettleton had clearly been instrumental, first in launching the Yellowstone Park campaign itself, and later, in securing public sympathy to retain the park until significant numbers of tourists could in fact begin visiting its wonders.

After 1883, the Northern Pacific Railroad spared no expense to promote Yellowstone National Park. As early as 1886, for example, it underwrote the construction of a series of hotels located near primary attractions. Charles S. Fee, general passenger agent in St. Paul, Minnesota, sought to publicize both the railroad and its accommodations by commissioning a

Yellowstone's Giant Geyser, from the pages of Wonderland, *1900. Courtesy of the Pacific Northwest Collection, University of Washington Libraries, Seattle.*

The rustic Old Faithful Inn, like its neighbor and namesake, Old Faithful Geyser, is still a popular attraction of the Upper Geyser Basin in Yellowstone National Park. This most famous of Yellowstone hotels was designed by the architect Robert C. Reamer, and completed in 1904 at a cost to the Northern Pacific Railroad of two hundred thousand dollars. Yellowstone National Park photograph (14476). Courtesy of the National Park Service.

colorfully written and illustrated series of guidebooks, beginning with his personal compilation, *Northern Pacific Railroad: The Wonderland Route to the Pacific Coast, 1885.*

By utilizing quotations from articulate travelers and well-known personalities, these guidebooks introduced Americans not only to Yellowstone, but to Mount Rainier, the Columbia River Gorge, the Cascade Mountains, and similar landmarks made accessible via the Northern Pacific. Even at this early date, Mount St. Helens, visible from the trains approaching Portland, Oregon, was featured for its appeal to observers as "the great Sugar Loaf" of the Pacific Northwest.

Obviously, what modern Americans would recognize as ecological awareness was rarely evident in these guidebook testimonials. After all, the primary objective was to publicize those features of the West which were experiencing growing popularity among tourists. More visitors, in turn, promised the Northern Pacific Railroad greater revenues from hotels, transcontinental trains, and its other passenger-related operations.

Commercial motives aside, the long-range impact of this publicity on the preservation movement in the United States was positive and significant. The railroad's dependence on unspoiled scenery to attract tourists tempered its purely extractive aims, such as logging, mining, and land development. The

"Mount St. Helens from Portland," caption and photo-illustration from Wonderland, 1902. *Courtesy of the Pacific Northwest Collection, University of Washington Libraries, Seattle.*

passenger department, at the very least, became one of the first and most outspoken defenders of Yellowstone National Park. Barely had the railroad come to the gates of the wonderland than Charles S. Fee declared on behalf of his employers:

We do not want to see the Falls of the Yellowstone driving the looms of a cotton factory, or

26

The Wonderland *guidebooks, published annually by the Northern Pacific Railroad, featured articles and photographs of western scenery and train travel. In the* Wonderland *cover for 1897, "Liberty" and the eagle float serenely above the Grand* Canyon and Lower Falls of Yellowstone. The 1899 cover symbolizes the bountiful harvests along the railroad routes. Courtesy of the Pacific Northwest Collection, University of Washington Libraries, Seattle.

the great geysers boiling pork for some gigantic packing-house, but in all the native majesty and grandeur in which they appear to-day, without, as yet, a single trace of that adornment which is desecration, that improvement which is equivalent to ruin, or that utilization which means utter destruction.

As if to underscore the pledge, in 1893 the Northern Pacific adopted a new logo, patterned after the Chinese yin-yang symbol of the balanced universe, and suspended it above the caption, "Yellowstone Park Line."

By the turn of the century, as interest in wildlife conservation grew in importance, representatives of the Northern Pacific again spoke out strongly in defense of Yellowstone. More Americans now recognized that the protection of natural wonders, as opposed to wild animals, required only limited amounts of land. Wildlife populations paid no heed to park boundaries laid out to preserve scenery, but instead seasonally followed their traditional migration routes. For the first time, Yellowstone's ecological shortcomings were dramatically apparent.

Left: *In addition to publicizing the national parks, the western railroads also highlighted natural wonders, such as the Columbia River Gorge, visible from their main line passenger trains. Reprinted by permission of Burlington Northern Inc.*

Despite its great size, the park lacked sufficient territory to protect its larger mammals, particularly elk, deer, and antelope. Every autumn, as these species deserted the park for their winter ranges in the lower elevations, they were forced to run a gauntlet of poachers and sportsmen who had no respect for bag limits. For Yellowstone to support its native wildlife effectively, either the park would have to be greatly enlarged or the animals themselves better protected when wandering outside its borders.

The Northern Pacific, through another of its authors, Olin D. Wheeler, enthusiastically supported both park expansion and wildlife protection measures. "In order ... to properly preserve these fast-disappearing relics of wild animal life to future generations," Wheeler wrote in the *Wonderland* guidebook for 1902, "additional territory should be added either to the park proper or to the forest reserve about it, so that absolute protection can be maintained...." Poachers and "game hogs" cared "only for their own selfish pleasure in killing as many deer or elks as they can," he bitterly noted. Perhaps the only solution lay in "the boys and girls" of America, those with the greatest stake in the destiny of Yellowstone. Wheeler concluded that from their

Right: The Northern Pacific Railroad's support of Yellowstone National Park as a breeding ground for big game heightened the awareness of hunters, fishermen, and tourists that the West was a great refuge for wildlife. Reprinted by permission of Burlington Northern Inc.

"irresistible" efforts, their "vim and enthusiasm," might spring the "national movement," a movement that would finally compel Congress to "arrange for game protection in the Yellowstone Park region for all future time."

Actually, another half century would pass before the addition of Jackson Hole to Grand Teton National Park, lying just to the south, complemented Yellowstone as a wildlife preserve. Again, the delay did not compromise the significance of that first crucial step —of stating unequivocally the need for park expansion. Through its agent, Olin D. Wheeler, the Northern Pacific Railroad fully shared in the credit for that endorsement.

Meanwhile, the national park idea was winning converts nationwide; at the turn of the century, Mount Rainier in Washington state was among the natural wonders proposed for park status. The Northern Pacific Railroad played a major role in establishing this reserve as well. Approved by Congress in 1899, the park was carved from square-mile sections on the peak; alternate sections were owned by the Northern Pacific, and the balance by the federal government. The railroad's sections dated back to its original land grant, awarded in 1864. Agreeing that these properties were best suited for scenic enjoyment, the government exchanged with Northern Pacific federally held public lands elsewhere in the Pacific Northwest.

The merits of the exchange were somewhat controversial, however. Historians have noted, for example, that the railroad seemed eager to forfeit its commercially worthless holdings on Mount Rainier, especially in light of the richly forested lands received in exchange for the peak. It is also probable, of course, that without the exchange there would not have been a park of any kind, at least not as early as 1899. Instead, much like the modern example of Mount St. Helens, Mount Rainier also would have entered the twentieth century as a checkerboard of properties. Because of the exchange, Mount Rainier was spared any possible conflicts over jurisdiction and, subsequently, it became a national park that much sooner.

Irrespective of complete federal ownership after 1899, the Northern Pacific had no intention of ignoring Mount Rainier as a spectacular tourist attraction. Throughout the 1890s, prospective travelers were lavishly introduced to Mount Rainier through the *Wonderland* series of guidebooks; after the park itself was created, the Northern Pacific Railroad promoted it to the benefit of both the government and the tourist industry.

For obvious reasons—primarily the sheer number and stunning diversity of its natural wonders—Yellowstone remained the premier attraction for the Northern Pacific well into the twentieth century. Between 1883 and 1902, tourists detrained several

Mount Rainier from Eunice Lake.
Courtesy of the National Park Service Branch
of Graphics Research, Springfield, Virginia.

Stagecoaches meeting the train at Gardiner Station, Montana, northern gateway to Yellowstone National Park, 1904. Robert C. Reamer, the architect of the Old Faithful Inn, also designed this Northern Pacific Railroad station. Yellowstone National Park photograph (64,662). Courtesy of the National Park Service.

miles north of the park at Cinnabar, Montana; by 1903 the spur line from Livingston had been extended to the park boundary at Gardiner. From there, it was only five miles by stagecoach to Mammoth Hot Springs, the first of the grand hotels on the park circuit. The Gardiner depot, designed by the Seattle architect Robert C. Reamer, was itself a striking combination of rustic logs, massive stone fireplaces, and high, beamed ceilings. But then, everything had to be first class, for only the wealthy could begin to afford the extravagance of traveling in a transcontinental Pullman or lounging in luxury hotels.

Democracy in the form of the automobile eventually would clamor at the gates of Yellowstone; before middle-class Americans took over the national parks, however, these scenic wonders would first be usurped by the railroads on behalf of their well-to-do clientele. Of the 51,895 visitors who entered Yellowstone during the summer of 1915, for example, fully 44,477 arrived by rail as opposed to only 7,418 by car. Just fifteen years later, however, the proportion had been completely reversed. In 1930 only 26,845 people used the rail entrances into Yellowstone in contrast to the 194,771 who entered by private automobile.

By 1930 no less than five major railroads served Yellowstone and its immediate vicinity. Their commitment to passenger traffic, despite the competition

The palatial National Hotel at Mammoth Hot Springs, Yellowstone, shown here around the turn of the century, was constructed in 1883 and later torn down in 1935. E. B. Thompson Collection (74-336). Courtesy of the National Park Service.

Automobiles meet Yellowstone-bound passengers beside the train at Gardiner, Montana, in June 1930. Only fifteen years earlier, trains and stagecoaches had enjoyed a virtual monopoly of national park patronage. Yellowstone National Park photograph (8082-4). Courtesy of the National Park Service.

of the automobile, is easily explained. Simply, although the proportion of rail travelers declined in comparison to auto vacationers, by 1925 the actual number of railroad patrons had recovered to its pre-World War I average. Until the Great Depression tightened its grip on rail passenger traffic in the early 1930s, approximately 40,000 people annually still went to "Wonderland" by train. No motivation among the western railroads for seeking to duplicate this ridership elsewhere was more compelling than the example set by the Northern Pacific—catalyst of the national park idea and first monopolizer of the "Yellowstone Park Line."

This Northern Pacific Railroad photograph shows the arrival of three hundred college students at Gardiner Gateway to take summer jobs in Yellowstone Park hotels, lodges, and camps. A fleet of park buses meets them at the station, ca. 1940. Courtesy of Burlington Northern Inc.

TRAINS *of* DISCOVERY

· C H A P T E R ·

2

The Santa Fe Railway's first train to the South Rim of the Grand Canyon, September 18, 1901. Courtesy of the Santa Fe Railway Company.

Thomas Moran's Grand Canyon, *purchased by the Santa Fe Railway in 1914, today forms the nucleus of the com-* *pany's world-renowned Collection of Southwestern Art. Courtesy of the Santa Fe Railway Company.*

PRESERVATION EXPRESS
Glacier, the Grand Canyon, and the National Park Service

When I first heard of the Santa Fe trains running to the edge of the Grand Cañon of Arizona, I was troubled with thoughts of the disenchantment likely to follow. But last winter, when I saw those trains crawling along through the pines of the Coconino Forest and close up to the brink of the chasm at Bright Angel, I was glad to discover that in the presence of such stupendous scenery they are nothing. The locomotives and trains are mere beetles and caterpillars, and the noise they make is as little disturbing as the hooting of an owl in the lonely woods.

John Muir, *Century Magazine*, November 1902

SOON AFTER the turn of the century, every major western railroad was playing a crucial role in the establishment, protection, and improvement of national parks. The managers of these lines were motivated more by a desire to promote tourism and increase profits than by altruism or environmental concern. Nevertheless, preservationists like John Muir came to recognize the value of forming an alliance with a powerful corporate group committed to similar goals, if not from similar ideals. Tourism at the time, however encouraged, provided the national parks with a solid economic justification

for their existence. No argument was more vital in a nation still unwilling to pursue scenic preservation at the cost of business achievement.

The Northern Pacific, as the first company to become involved with the national parks, set an example for the other railroads to follow. Across the West, railroad companies learned to appreciate the publicity and profits that could be won by sponsoring scenic preservation in their particular spheres of influence. Among the earliest to respond to the opportunity was the Southern Pacific Railroad in California, which lobbied in 1890 for the establishment of Yosemite, Sequoia, and General Grant national parks, all located in the High Sierra. "Even the soulless Southern Pacific R.R. Co., never counted on for anything good, helped nobly in pushing the bill for [Yosemite] park through Congress." With these words, John Muir recorded the initial astonishment among preservation interests.

Indeed, the company rose to become one of the most vigorous sponsors of protecting natural scenery in general and the West Coast national parks in particular. In 1898, for example, the Southern Pacific's passenger department was the original founder of *Sunset* magazine, a monthly periodical designed expressly to entice settlement and tourism to states served by the railroad, especially California. Each issue contained lavish illustrations, highly descriptive articles, and romantic advertisements promoting Yosemite Valley, the Giant Sequoias, and other national park attractions accessible via Southern Pacific passenger trains. One of the most popular subjects for photographers was the Wawona Tunnel Tree in Yosemite's Mariposa Redwood Grove. With such wonders of nature to induce travel, the Southern Pacific Railroad profited from the national parks of California for many years.

The Grand Canyon of Arizona provided the Atchison, Topeka & Santa Fe Railway with a similar golden opportunity. Travel to the canyon was considerably improved with the completion in 1901 of a spur track to the South Rim from Williams, Arizona, a distance of approximately sixty miles. Visitors were no longer forced to endure long and tiring stagecoach rides in the desert heat. Similarly, in January 1905, the Santa Fe dedicated its luxurious El Tovar Hotel, also on the canyon brink. Here, too, the publicity of the railroad and its structural improvements contributed immeasurably to the protection of the Grand Canyon, for not until 1908 was it set aside as a national monument by order of President Theodore Roosevelt.

The Santa Fe Railway expected the national monument to focus greater attention on the Grand Canyon and, like the designation of Yellowstone as a "national park," to arouse the curiosity of literally millions of Americans. If these competing western railroads were to approach either the success or the prestige of the Northern Pacific, then Yellowstone was the model they had to recreate.

No railroad, however, was more determined to compete with its rivals than the Great Northern Railway. Completed in 1893 by James J. Hill, it paralleled the Northern Pacific from Minnesota to Washington, except that Hill chose a right-of-way much closer to the Canadian border. As a result, the Great Northern bypassed the Yellowstone country by more than two hundred miles and instead pierced the jagged ranges of the Rocky Mountains in the northwestern corner of Montana.

This 1904 advertisement informed easterners about the natural wonders of the West by comparing the exaggerated height of the Wawona Tunnel Tree with the famous Flatiron Building in New York City. Reprinted by permission of the Southern Pacific Transportation Company.

The Wawona Tunnel Tree in the Mariposa Redwood Grove of Yosemite Park is featured on the cover of this 1904 Southern Pacific Railroad brochure. Carved out in 1881, the tree finally toppled during the harsh winter of 1969. Courtesy of the California State Railroad Museum, Sacramento.

The El Tovar Hotel, built on the South Rim of Arizona's Grand Canyon by the Santa Fe Railway, is a classic example of railroad promotion of the national parks. Named for the Spanish explorer Pedro de Tovar, the hotel opened on January 14, 1905. Thereafter it was operated by the Fred Harvey Company, a name renowned since 1876 for dining and hotel service along the Atchison, Topeka & Santa Fe right-of-way. This rendering of the hotel by the artist Louis Akin was purchased by the Santa Fe Railway in 1907. Courtesy of the Santa Fe Railway Company Collection of Southwestern Art.

As early as 1901, the noted explorer and sportsman, George Bird Grinnell, endorsed government protection of this region as a forest preserve, describing it for *Century Magazine* as "the Crown of the Continent." "Here," he observed, "are cañons deeper and narrower than those of the Yellowstone, mountains higher than those of the Yosemite." In other words, properly protected and developed, the territory was equally worthy of national park status. James J. Hill, renowned for his skepticism about rail passenger service, did not seem very interested. Then, in 1907, his son, Louis W. Hill, was appointed president of the Great Northern Railway. Louis, on the other hand, did sense this magnificent opportunity: after all, immediately south of the region Grinnell had described ran the tracks of the railroad's main line.

The following year, Congress began debating the merits of a national park bill. As prospects for its passage improved, Hill's initial interest swelled into unbridled enthusiasm. For years, the Montana Rockies had been out of reach to all but a few hardy sportsmen. Now that a national park might actually hug the tracks of the Great Northern, this trickle of visitors could conceivably be turned into a flood. Perhaps, Hill mused, even Yellowstone might be forced to sacrifice some of its popularity to its newest competitor. Meanwhile, as part of his railroad's ongoing "See America First" campaign, Hill noted that Americans were encouraged to spend their travel dollars elsewhere—in the Swiss Alps or the Canadian Rockies, for example—simply because equally spectacular landscapes at home were not properly protected and promoted.

Swayed by the argument, Congress approved and, in May of 1910, the president signed the act establishing Glacier National Park. With the park itself a reality, Hill's next course of action was obvious: he must do everything possible to provide for the accommodation of visitors. Personally, he did not care to commit the Great Northern both to the construction and operation of a hotel chain. At best, the park season would be only three months long; the project offered little prospect of breaking even on such a substantial capital investment. Yet, Hill realized that he had little choice. Luxury accommodations were the prerequisite for attracting visitors to the national parks, especially in the days before the widespread use of automobiles, when only wealthier Americans could afford a vacation in the West. In any case, every extra passenger who filled an otherwise empty seat on one of the railroad's existing transcontinental trains would represent a net profit, inasmuch as the costs of operating a train were unchanged regardless of the number of people using the system.

In addition to the practical considerations that inevitably crossed Hill's mind, there loomed an

Louis W. Hill (left), *president of the Great Northern Railway, was instrumental in the creation and development of Glacier National Park. He is shown here in front of the Glacier Park Lodge at East Glacier Park Station, ca. 1920. Courtesy of Burlington Northern Inc.*

equally compelling vision. Louis W. Hill took great personal pride in opening Glacier National Park as his own unique gift to the nation. From the outset, visitors to the park detected his dedication to the project. Mary Roberts Rinehart, for example, writing for *Collier's* magazine, informed her readers in 1916: "Were it not for the Great Northern Railway, travel through Glacier Park would be practically impossible." Of course, the railroad was "not entirely altruistic," the popular novelist confessed, "and yet I believe that Mr. Louis Warren Hill, known always as 'Louie' Hill, has had an ideal and followed it—followed it with an enthusiasm that is contagious."

Proof of her contention could be seen throughout the backcountry, where Hill had scattered a striking assortment of Swiss-style alpine chalets. But nowhere was his commitment more grandly displayed than at East Glacier Park Station and Many Glacier, on the banks of Swiftcurrent Lake. At these locations, dipping lavishly into regional resources of timber and stone, Hill had personally supervised the construction of two sprawling, rustic hotels, each constituting a $500,000 investment. "Glacier Park Hotel . . . is almost as large as the National Capitol at Washington," Rinehart observed, displaying a slight tendency to exaggerate. Still, the structure was impressive, and in combination with its counterpart at Many Glacier, it moved her to reemphasize that the management of the Great Northern Railway "has done more than anything else to make the park possible for tourists."

Although as much credit could be given to any of the other western railroads, Hill devoted a unique degree of personal involvement to the national parks. His spirit fired the national preservation movement at this very critical juncture in its history. His efforts to improve Glacier coincided with a twofold campaign to protect the national parks from damaging encroachments and, equally important, to

The alpine splendor of Swiftcurrent Lake in Glacier National Park inspired the Great Northern Railway to design Many Glacier Hotel, reminiscent of a lodge in Switzerland. Courtesy of Burlington Northern Inc.

Top Left: *The* Empire Builder *arrives at Glacier Park Station, 1934. George A. Grant photograph (924). Courtesy of the National Park Service.* Top Right: *Opened in 1913, the Glacier Park Lodge displayed Native American and Oriental motifs. Hileman photograph (79G-29A-5). Courtesy of the National Archives, Washington, D.C.* Above: *The site of the lodge was purchased from the Piegan Indians. Hileman photograph (79G-29A-1). Courtesy of the National Archives.*

establish a National Park Service. In California, preservationists had just lost a bitter fight to save the Hetch Hetchy Valley within Yosemite National Park from being turned over to the city of San Francisco for its municipal water supply. The loss of Hetch Hetchy's inviting meadows and woodlands to a dam and reservoir stunned the Sierra Club and its supporters; never before, they concluded, had the need been more critical for a National Park Service to defend the land.

Under the existing arrangement, the Department of the Interior, the War Department, and the U. S. Forest Service all shared responsibility for managing the reserves. No single, centralized federal agency had the power to protect the national parks as a system. But how, preservationists asked themselves, could such an agency be established, especially over the objections of existing federal departments, each jealous of its own authority?

Meanwhile, preservationists were confronted by a powerful numbers argument. Proponents of the Hetch Hetchy dam had been quick to point out that only a few hundred "nature lovers" enjoyed the valley during the summer months; in contrast, fully half a million San Franciscans would benefit year-round from the reservoir. Lacking a rationale whose emotional appeal was equally persuasive, preservationists found themselves in an extremely vulnerable position. The geography of tourism was also against

them. Every national park, including Yosemite, was in the West, far removed from the centers of population. Finally, only a few Americans were sympathetic with purely ecological justifications for scenic preservation. John Muir, whose California-based Sierra Club led the fight against the dam, concluded sadly: "Nothing dollarable is safe, however guarded."

Only the railroads, whose own desire to boost travel to the national parks did not materially compromise their scenic integrity, seemed even remotely sympathetic with preservationist ideals. It followed that preservation groups needed to strengthen their ties with the railroads. Richard B. Watrous, secretary of the American Civic Association, and Allen Chamberlain, a leading activist of the Appalachian Mountain Club, were among the first to publicize the advantages of such an alliance. According to Chamberlain, the Hetch Hetchy debate was an especially compelling example of the need to work even harder "to stimulate public interest in the national parks by talking more about their possibilities as vacation resorts." Only if more Americans "could be induced to visit these scenic treasure houses," he concluded, would the public "come to appreciate their value and stand firmly in their defense."

Groping for his own analogy, Watrous decided that tourism might best be defined as the "dignified exploitation of our national parks." Accordingly, in 1911, he urged preservation groups nationwide to

publicize "the direct material returns that will accrue to the railroads, to the concessionaires, and to the various sections of the country that will benefit by increased travel." The railroads' support, he concluded, was particularly "essential" as "one of those practical phases of making the aesthetic possible."

It remained for Secretary of the Interior Walter L. Fisher to give these views the sanction of the government. In September of 1911, he convened a special national parks conference at Yellowstone to discuss the major problems facing the reserves. When several prominent executives of the western railroads, including Louis W. Hill of the Great Northern, accepted Fisher's invitation to attend, preservationists were convinced they were being heard. Fisher's introductory remarks were equally heartening. Speaking directly to the railroad executives, he praised their support for the national parks as the highest form of "enlightened selfishness," self-interest of the type entitling it to the "grateful recognition" of all park advocates. One after another, the executives, led by Hill, returned the compliment with further promises to assist the government in upgrading the facilities of the national parks, espe-

Left: *Alpine adventurers in Glacier National Park highlight this 1927 advertisement. Reprinted by permission of Burlington Northern Inc.*

cially hotels, roads, and trails. As so many preservationists had hoped, the Yellowstone conference of 1911 established beyond a doubt the firm commitment of the western railroads to embark upon national park improvements and publicity campaigns.

The support could not have been more timely; the National Park Service bill, introduced to Congress in 1911, ran into stiff opposition from powerful opponents in the federal bureaucracy. As a result, hearings on the legislation were still being held five years later. Only the endorsement of the western railroads seemed unshaken. Much like the preservationist interests, the railroads looked forward to working with a single government agency, one committed to promoting the parks full-time rather than as a sideline to a more compelling—and often conflicting—management philosophy.

Meanwhile, the railroads engaged in a flurry of national park promotion; as a group, they spent hundreds of thousands of dollars on advertising brochures, complimentary park guidebooks, and full-page magazine spreads, some of which were in dramatic full-color. Fortunately for park visitors, the competition among the railroads was occasionally tempered by some cooperation. With the arrival of the Union Pacific at the western boundary of Yellowstone National Park in 1907, the Northern Pacific Railroad finally lost its monopoly over the area. Similarly, by 1915, the Chicago, Burlington & Quincy had

From original painting by Adolph Heinze
THE HIGHWAY NEAR MANY GLACIER HOTEL

This is modern travel in an unspoiled wilderness. Each mile on these highways opens up new vistas of beauty and each turn in the road leads to a new adventure.

This colorful painting of limousine travel in Glacier National Park enticed readers of the Great Northern Railway guidebook, The Call of the Mountains, *ca. 1927. Courtesy of the Pacific Northwest Collection, University of Washington Libraries, Seattle.*

access to Yellowstone via Cody, Wyoming, a two-hour drive due east of the reserve. Thanks in large part to Stephen T. Mather, who, in December of 1914, became the assistant secretary of the interior in charge of national parks, travelers to Yellowstone finally were able to interchange their routes of entry and departure, all on the same railroad ticket.

Mather, who had already made his own fortune in the mining of borax, now rose to the challenge of bringing order to the national park system. As a Californian and a member of the Sierra Club, his business background and conservation experience taught him that publicity was still the key to winning more public support for the reserves. Accordingly, he nurtured the alliance between preservationists and western railroad officials at every opportunity. The lines' financial response continued to be substantial, with the expectation that their investments would stimulate the flow of goodwill in both directions. In this vein, the Santa Fe and Union Pacific railroads jointly spent half a million dollars in 1915 on national park displays at the Panama-Pacific International Exposition in San Francisco. The Union Pacific contributed a full-size replica of the lobby of the Old Faithful Inn and Old Faithful Geyser in Yellowstone: every hour the modeled "wonder" erupted in a jet of water, just like the original more than a thousand miles away. Visitors were obviously delighted by this unusual display, and equally important from the railroad's perspective, the exhibit reminded people of the national parks' beauty and how they might be reached.

Stimulating public awareness of the available transportation to and the extraordinary scenery of national parks was also the purpose of the *National Parks Portfolio,* a stunning publicity volume containing pictures and descriptions of all the major preserves. No less than seventeen of the western railroads contributed $43,000 in 1916 toward publication of the first edition. Afterward, Stephen T. Mather supervised the mailing of 275,000 copies of the collector's item to carefully selected scholars, politicians, chambers of commerce officials, newspaper editors, and other American leaders who were likely to boost the national park idea.

Meanwhile, with the passage of the National Park Service bill still in doubt, preservationists welcomed another major railroad to their fold of active political allies. This was the Chicago, Burlington & Quincy. The approval in 1915 of Rocky Mountain National Park, sixty miles northwest of the Burlington's terminus in Denver, Colorado, had provided a special incentive for the company to endorse the creation of a National Park Service. The Burlington began to promote Cody, Wyoming, and the Cody Road as the most scenic gateway into Yellowstone. Finally, an agreement with the Great Northern Railway enabled the Burlington to sell through-tickets to land-

Union Pacific

YOU COULD EASILY LOSE A GREAT CITY IN THIS CHASM

GRAND CANYON NATIONAL PARK

Be sure you see it this Wonderful New Way—

Nowhere on the face of the globe is there anything like it. Even when you see it — and stand gazing over the lofty North Rim from Grand Canyon Lodge — even then it is too vast to comprehend!

It is literally true that if some great city were set down in this 250 mile long chasm, its presence could easily be overlooked. The tallest buildings in America would be dwarfed to insignificance beside its mighty temples.

Everyone should see it! No doubt you too, like every true American, have resolved to visit this greatest of American wonders. Here is a new way to do it — an exclusive Union Pacific tour which brings you to the Canyon by a new route, through the amazing colorful and wholly different canyon-region of southern Utah — leading to Grand Canyon as a climax.

All this wonderful tour can easily be included in a two weeks' vacation trip, the tour of the canyons requiring only five days by motor-bus after leaving your Pullman at Cedar City, the gateway. First comes Zion National Park, with its tremendous towers of painted stone! Then Bryce Canyon, a new National Park, a place of cream and coral rocks carved in the shape of castles, cathedrals, gods and men! And finally Grand Canyon, with wild Cedar Breaks and deer-filled Kaibab Forest along the way.

You may go independently, or on an Escorted All-Expense Tour, with interesting companions. The cost is surprisingly low. No other trip offers so much at so little expense, and with such economy of time. The season is June 1 to October 1. Send the coupon at once for richly illustrated booklet and full details.

C. J. Collins, General Passenger Agent, Dept. 329
Union Pacific System, Omaha, Neb.
Please send me complete information including cost, and booklet about Zion-Bryce Canyon-Grand Canyon National Parks. I am also interested in:
☐ Pacific Northwest and Alaska   ☐ Yellowstone
☐ Colorado   ☐ California   ☐ Dude Ranches
☐ Escorted All-Expense Tours   ☐ Hawaii
If student, state age.... and grade....
Name_____
Street_____
City_____State_____

Union Pacific
THE OVERLAND ROUTE

Union Pacific

COME VIA GLORIOUS ZION CANYON TO SUBLIME GRAND CANYON

And also see

BRYCE CANYON NATIONAL PARK
CEDAR BREAKS
KAIBAB NAT'L FOREST

The Grand Canyon is the most stupendous chasm on the globe. It overpowers by sheer immensity. But Zion and Bryce Canyons are equally thrilling—some believe even more beautiful—in entirely different ways.

The walls of Zion Canyon are cut into tremendous temples and towers, rising sheer four-fifths of a mile into the blue Utah sky. There is nothing like them for sheer depth and vivid color anywhere on earth.

Bryce Canyon is wholly unique—an enchanted Oriental city. Its walls are fluted like a gigantic organ; it holds great temples, pagodas and cathedrals, and endless sculptures of human and animal shapes, startlingly real! And the colors range from delicate cream and coral to flaming orange and vermilion.

Come to Grand Canyon this summer by this wonderful new way! Zion, Bryce and Grand Canyon are all easily included in a two weeks' vacation trip—with every convenience of modern travel, and *at surprisingly low cost.* The tour of the canyons, stopping at handsome new lodges, requires only five days by motor-bus after leaving your Pullman at Cedar City, the gateway. You can go independently or by an Escorted All-Expense Tour with interesting companions.

Season: June 1 to October 1. Send the coupon today for richly illustrated booklet and full details.

The Great White Throne, Zion Canyon

C. J. Collins, General Passenger Agent, Dept. 317
Union Pacific System, Omaha, Neb.
Please send me complete information including cost, and booklet about Zion-Bryce Canyon-Grand Canyon National Parks. I am also interested in:
☐ Pacific Northwest and Alaska   ☐ Yellowstone
☐ Colorado   ☐ California   ☐ Dude Ranches
☐ Escorted All-Expense Tours   ☐ Hawaii
If student state grade.
Name_____Street_____
City_____State_____

Union Pacific
THE OVERLAND ROUTE

Union Pacific Railroad advertisements, 1929, reprinted with permission.

Stephen T. Mather, the first director of the National Park Service, is pictured here above the "drumhead" of the observation car on the North Coast Limited, *the premier passenger train of the Northern Pacific Railroad, ca. 1925. Photograph (79-PGN-385), courtesy of the National Archives, Washington, D.C.*

marks farther west, including Glacier and Mount Rainier national parks.

Similar arrangements among the Burlington's competitors were offered as a sign of good faith, as another expression of their sincere hope that a National Park Service would soon be established. In this new spirit of cooperation, P. S. Eustis, general passenger agent of the Chicago, Burlington & Quincy, concluded five years of hearings on the National Park Service bill before the House Committee on the Public Lands. "We offer every diversity of route possible," he testified, "all on one ticket."

Two additional national park conferences, called in 1912 and 1915 by the Department of the Interior, likewise reaffirmed the unanimous support for a Park Service among the western railroads. The opposition in the federal bureaucracy, once confident of success, could no longer withstand this powerful tide of enthusiasm from such a prestigious quarter. On August 25, 1916, preservationists cleared their last potential hurdle when President Woodrow Wilson signed the National Park Service Act into law.

In recognition of his many contributions to the national parks in his capacity as assistant secretary of the interior, Stephen T. Mather was appointed the first director of the new organization. With the National Park Service a reality, he now turned his attention to park system additions and improvements. Mather was particularly concerned about the Southwest, where scenic magnificence was represented by only one major reserve, the Grand Canyon. Subsequently, in 1919, he won approval for Zion National Park, the spectacular gorge in southern Utah renowned as "The Yosemite of the Desert." Bryce Canyon, a neighboring wonderland of fanciful spires and sandstone gargoyles, eventually received park status in 1924.

Neither area, however, had adequate roads or overnight accommodations. Cedar Breaks, soon to become the breathtaking national monument between Bryce and Zion, and the North Rim of the Grand Canyon, approximately one hundred miles to the south, were in the same predicament. To alleviate these problems of transportation and lodging, Mather approached the president and board of directors of the Union Pacific Railroad and asked them to take charge of the needs of tourists throughout the entire region.

The Union Pacific, despite some initial reluctance to commit itself to such a substantial investment, eventually responded with everything Mather had hoped for—and more. Accompanied by widespread advertising campaigns in the best tradition of national park promotion, the railroad constructed a new branch line from Lund, on the Los Angeles/Salt Lake City main line, over to Cedar City, just north of Zion. At Cedar City, passengers transferred to company-supplied buses for package tours of all four of the area's "wonderlands." To accommodate the many expected guests, the Union Pacific constructed

Union Pacific Railroad advertisement, 1927, reprinted with permission.

BRYCE CANYON

Colorful ·· Colossal ·· Sublime

Bryce Canyon—Grand Canyon National Park
Zion National Park—Kaibab Forest—Cedar Breaks

Season June 1 to October 1

In Bryce Canyon are immense chasms filled with realistic rock forms resembling ruined Oriental cities and castles and cathedrals of the Middle Ages, and with statues of men and beasts, all glowing with many colors. This region also includes tremendous colored canyons, colossal buttes, prismatic plains, vast virgin forests, wild horses, countless deer, mysterious cliff dwellings.

See them all this summer. Easy to reach. Low summer fares. Through Pullmans to Cedar City, Utah, thence 3, 4 or 5-day all-expense motor-bus tours; also escorted tours. Comfortable lodges. Miles of scenic trails. A memorable vacation itself or a side trip en route to Yellowstone or the Pacific Coast. *The Zion—Grand Canyon Red Book tells all, free for the asking.*

Address nearest representative or General Passenger Agent, Dept. 119, at Omaha, Neb. : Salt Lake City, Utah : Portland, Oregon : Los Angeles, Calif.

UNION PACIFIC
THE OVERLAND ROUTE

GRAND CANYON

"Most Sublime of All Earthly Scenes"

Grand Canyon National Park

So world travelers say of this colossal chasm, more than a mile deep, more than two hundred miles long, and twelve miles wide, filled with magnificent rock temples aflame with changing colors. See it this summer from the lofty North Rim, reached through the enchanting Kaibab National Forest with its thousands of deer, by a 5-day, all-expense Union Pacific motor bus tour that also includes

Zion National Park
Bryce Canyon   Cedar Breaks
Kaibab Forest   Prismatic Plains

Easy to reach. Low summer fares. Through Pullmans to Cedar City, Utah, the gateway. Independent and Escorted tours. Comfortable lodges. A wonderful vacation itself or a memorable side trip en route to Yellowstone or the Pacific Coast. Season June 1 to October 1.

The Zion-Grand Canyon Red Book tells all. Ask for it.

Address nearest representative or General Passenger Agent, Dept. 142, at Omaha, Neb. : Salt Lake City, Utah : Portland, Ore. : Los Angeles, Calif.

UNION PACIFIC
THE OVERLAND ROUTE

Union Pacific Railroad advertisements, 1927, reprinted with permission.

lodges and cabins in each reserve. The most elegant of these buildings, the Grand Canyon Lodge on the North Rim, was dedicated in 1928. For the first time since 1905, when the Santa Fe Railway opened the El Tovar on the South Rim, both sides of the canyon had comparable service.

"Our relations with the parks are naturally very close, and I believe they should be closer," said Louis W. Hill in defense of his own $1.5 million investment in Glacier National Park. In fact, his hotels and chalets, assigned to the railroad's subsidiary, Glacier Park, Inc., were not sold until 1961. Managed today by the Greyhound Corporation, the buildings are still there, rising against their mountain backgrounds, blending the man-made with the natural in a fitting memorial to Hill's idealism and philanthropy.

Stephen Mather's death in 1930 brought to an end more than two decades of dedicated involvement with America's national parks, yet his primary goal to increase park visitation had been achieved. More than three million people traveled through the national parks and monuments that year, almost a tenfold increase since he had taken office as director of the National Park Service. Railroad executives applauded his success, as did most preservationists, who rejoiced in the security that popularity brought to the scenic reserves.

The alliance forged by the western railroads, preservation groups, and the National Park Service survived intact for the next quarter century. As late as 1960, the pages of *Holiday, National Geographic,* and similar magazines sparkled with advertisements depicting the joys of rediscovering the West by rail, especially by visiting the national parks. On the Santa Fe Railway, for example, the streamliner *Grand Canyon* provided daily service between Chicago and Los Angeles, with through-cars to the canyon by way of the spur track from Williams, Arizona. Similarly, the Union Pacific added the *National Parks Special* for seasonal traffic to Zion, Bryce, and the Grand Canyon; it also expanded service to include the *Yellowstone Special,* whose summer runs ferried patrons between West Yellowstone and connecting main line trains at Salt Lake City.

For this legacy to have survived into the modern era, passenger trains in the West would have had to dramatically increase their patronage. Instead, the passenger business barely broke even during the 1960s as the federal government invested billions of dollars in competing highways and airports rather than in railroad facilities. In addition, many of the railroads in the East were dismantling their passenger operations, depriving trains in the West of vital connections with major population centers. Consequently, the promotion of the national parks by the western railroads no longer seemed justified, and public awareness about that unique relationship and its history finally dimmed.

Passengers departing Union Pacific company hotels in the South-west were treated to employee "sing aways." Here employees of the Bryce Canyon National Park Lodge sing good-bye to some summer guests in 1940. Courtesy of the Union Pacific Railroad Company Museum, Omaha, Nebraska.

Evidence during the early 1980s pointed to the restoration of rail transportation in the United States, not only between major cities, but to the national parks as well. Preservation groups were especially heartened in 1983 by the announcement that a private developer intended to purchase and rehabilitate the Santa Fe Railway branch line between Williams, Arizona, and the South Rim of the Grand Canyon. As late as August 1983 it appeared that the track would be torn up for scrap; finally, in the railroad's eleventh hour, a proposal for saving the branch line was endorsed by the Santa Fe Railway, the developer, and the town of Williams.

For its part, the Santa Fe Railway agreed to sell the tracks to the developer, Charles Newman, president of Railroad Resources Inc., for approximately three million dollars. Meanwhile, Williams agreed to allow Railroad Resources Inc., to construct a hotel complex within the community as part of a twenty million dollar project to connect Williams, the Grand Canyon airport, and facilities at the South Rim via the railroad. Early plans for the railroad itself called for purchasing a steam locomotive and vintage

A mile deep, miles wide, & painted like a sunset

That's the Grand Canyon of Arizona

For art booklets of the train and trip address
W. J. Black, Pass. Traffic Mgr.
A.T. & S.F. Ry. System,
1051 Railway Exchange, Chicago

You can go there in a Pullman to the rim at El Tovar, en route to Sunny California on the train of luxury

The California Limited

Santa Fe
All the way

Right: *Is she listening? Western railroads often encouraged the romantic aspect of the national parks, as demonstrated in this suggestive advertisement from the December 1910 issue of* McClure's. *Courtesy of the Santa Fe Railway Company.*

heavyweight passenger cars to ferry hotel patrons between Williams and the canyon rim.

Environmentalists, concerned about overcrowding in the national parks, greeted the announcement as a vindication of their contention that all future development of visitor services and overnight accommodations should occur outside the parks rather than next to their primary attractions. Similarly, rail passenger lobbyists endorsed the restoration as part of their own campaign to rehabilitate the rail passenger network dismantled throughout the United States during the 1960s. In this spirit both environmentalists and rail passenger advocates looked forward to another "pragmatic alliance," a union whose historical significance seemed on the verge of renewed importance in the pending resurrection of the route of the *Grand Canyon* to its former glory.

Right: *The El Tovar Hotel in 1936, overlooking the depths of Arizona's Grand Canyon. George A. Grant Collection (910). Courtesy of the National Park Service.*

TRAINS *of* DISCOVERY

· C H A P T E R ·

3

A Yosemite Valley Railroad train pulls out of the station at El Portal.
Courtesy of the National Park Service, Yosemite Collections.

The Santa Fe Railway acquired this painting of Yosemite Falls by Charles Rogers in 1911 to promote its connection to the Yosemite Valley Railroad. Courtesy of the Santa Fe Railway Company Collection of Southwestern Art.

YOSEMITE VALLEY RAILROAD
Highway of History, Pathway to Promise

The Yosemite Valley Railroad strikes for the National Park line from Merced. . . . Up its matchless canyon this new trail toils, unfolding moment by moment one of the most picturesque series of mountain pictures that nature has fashioned in her whole wide world. . . . This little piece of railroad is sure to take a leading place among the few famous scenic railways of the world. From the observation cars every change of scenery may be taken advantage of by the passenger in Summer without exposure to the dust and the rays of the California sun.

Lanier Bartlet, *Pacific Monthly*, 1907

If direct rail passenger service to the national parks in the United States is ever restored, rebuilding the Yosemite Valley Railroad undoubtedly would have high priority. Among wilderness enthusiasts, there might still be mixed emotions, much as was the case following completion of the line in May 1907. Edward H. Hamilton, correspondent for *Cosmopolitan* magazine, declared that some park visitors took the news "very much as if the Black Cavalry of Commerce has been sent out to trample down the fairy rings." "In California and the far West," he elaborated, "there are people who insist that hereafter the great valley is to be a mere picnic-ground with dancing-platforms, beery choruses, and couples contorting in the two-step." Such critics, however, should be dismissed as only "nature cranks" and the "athletic rich," those "stout pilgrims with long purses and no ailments." "There is the railroad into Yosemite," Hamilton remarked for emphasis, "and all the arguments since Adam and Eve will not put it away."

Actually, the Yosemite Valley Railroad did not enter the national park proper, nor were Hamilton's predictions, like his geographical information, free of miscalculation. Reportedly bankrupt in 1944, the line was sold at auction the following year and im-

63

Left: *The Yosemite Valley Railroad featured this detailed cover on its promotional brochure for the 1928 travel season. Courtesy of the National Park Service, Yosemite Collections.*

mediately scrapped. Today, only crumbling embankments and rotting wooden trestles stand as reminders of its former existence. Hamilton's so-called "nature cranks," also politely known as "purists," were misguided in their fears about the railway's impact on Yosemite National Park. Opposed to all types of construction in or near park areas, purists failed to recognize, as did the more moderate preservationists, that the railroads of the West were in fact among the strongest allies of scenic protection. Instead, it remained for the automobile, not the train and connecting motorcoach, to transform the most popular national parks into classic examples of what author Edward Abbey has denounced as "Industrial Tourism."

Constructed between September 1905 and May 1907, the Yosemite Valley Railroad ran from its western terminus at Merced to El Portal, approximately seventy-eight miles northeast through the mounting summits of the Sierra Nevada. The last two-thirds of the railway cut through the spectacular recesses of the Merced River Canyon. Finally, the railroad terminated when confronted by the impenetrable ramparts of the High Sierra, which form the western boundary of Yosemite National Park. Passengers

The Yosemite Valley Railroad's Flyer *strains the last few miles uphill through the Merced River Canyon to the station at El* *Portal, gateway to Yosemite National Park. Courtesy of the National Park Service, Yosemite Collections.*

then transferred to company-owned stagecoaches for the remaining twelve-mile journey to the valley floor. To facilitate the operation, the Yosemite Valley Railroad, not the federal government, provided the access road (now known as the Arch Rock entrance) across the park between El Portal and the valley proper.

In spite of its relatively high fares—$18.50 round-trip—the railroad thrived almost from the very beginning. Its initial competitor on the route, the stageline from Merced, went out of business as trains cut the ride to El Portal from a two-day ordeal to a four-hour delight. With the introduction of the first motorcoach service in 1913, the stage ride, which used to add another three or four hours to the journey, was dramatically improved. Thereafter, only an hour and thirty-five minutes was required to reach Yosemite from trackside at El Portal. For travelers arriving on the evening train, the railroad constructed the Del Portal, a luxurious four-story hotel, just a short distance from the station. Unfortunately, this truly rustic masterpiece was destroyed by fire only a decade after its dedication in 1907.

In rapid succession, the railroad introduced additional improvements for the pleasure and convenience of its passengers. In April 1909, for example, officials completed arrangements with the Southern Pacific Railroad for direct sleeping-car service from Los Angeles to El Portal, followed the next year by equivalent Pullman connections from San Francisco. These contracts enabled a patron purchasing a first-class ticket in either city to board a train in the evening, retire to the comfort of a berth, and wake up early the next morning at the gateway to Yosemite National Park, all without breaking slumber to change trains at Merced. For day travelers, the Yosemite Valley Railroad added a parlor-observation car to the trains, and, during the summer months, a completely equipped, full-sized diner.

This luxurious equipment, coupled with colorful advertising campaigns in major magazines and newspapers, steadily contributed to the popularity of the Yosemite Valley Railroad. The line achieved an important milestone in 1916, when its trains ferried 14,251 passengers to waiting motorcoaches at El Portal.

On a more disquieting note, 1916 also marked the first time in the history of Yosemite National Park that more people entered the reserve by automobile than by train. Almost immediately, highway travel surged at the expense of the Yosemite Valley Railroad. During 1917, the volume of train passengers to the park plummeted by almost forty percent to only 8,612 fares. The next year's patronage figures were even worse. Throughout the whole of 1918, fewer than 4,000 people saw the Merced River Canyon

Pullman Service *All the Way*

The end of your railroad journey and the entrance to the magic valley — that is El Portal. Here is the terminal station of Yosemite Valley Railroad, a distinctive rustic structure blending admirably with the rugged setting.

As the train nears Yosemite Valley, the view becomes ever more magnificent. Just before reaching El Portal—the river rushing by at our feet—in the hazy distance, a silvery shimmering streak breaking the rugged cliffs. It is Chinquapin Falls, first to be seen of the waterfalls of Yosemite—a promise of the scenic glories soon to be unfolded.

This page from the Yosemite Valley Railroad's 1928 travel brochure, "Yosemite via Merced Canyon Route," featured the station platform at El Portal. Courtesy of the National Park Service, Yosemite Collections.

The Del Portal Hotel, built by the Yosemite Valley Railroad in 1907, was located a short distance up the hill from the station at El Portal. Unfortunately, the hotel was destroyed by fire a decade later. Courtesy of the National Park Service, Yosemite Collections.

from the train, even though the round-trip coach fare was significantly reduced from $18.50 to $15.50 per passenger.

In contrast, that same year 26,669 people entered Yosemite Valley in automobiles, up from 14,527 and 22,456 in 1916 and 1917, respectively. Clearly, the American love affair with the horseless carriage was well under way. In its anxiety to encourage greater public use of the reserves, the National Park Service had no intention of cooling the romance, especially in Yosemite Valley, where auto-touring had already become the most popular form of sight-seeing. "The fact that the majority . . . of people entering the park came in private automobiles," reported the superintendent in 1917, "is evidence that it is this class of travel that must be given the bulk of consideration in future park development work." Specifically, "roads and public parking places must be given special consideration by the Service, and garage facilities and hotel and camp accommodations which appeal to this class of travel must be maintained by the concessioners."

This assessment, so conspicuously incompatible with the needs of today's Yosemite Valley, originally met with the approval of most preservation groups.

Right: *Southern Pacific Railroad advertisement, 1923. Courtesy of the National Park Service, Yosemite Collections.*

69

CRATER LAKE

OREGON'S
Mountain Playground

SOUTHERN PACIFIC

Just prior to World War I, when cars were first admitted to national parks, all of the reserves suffered from too little rather than too much tourism. For example, only 5,000 people visited Yosemite Valley in 1902, a figure that barely doubled even with the coming of the railroad. Statistics from the other national parks indicated much the same type of visitation problem. With good reason, therefore, preservationists feared for the integrity of the entire national park system. They realized that Congress was not about to support the parks indefinitely for the sole benefit of a small number of the American people, particularly when those people were wealthy enough to afford expensive railroad tickets and lodging in luxury hotels. To compound the problem, every national park was in the West, far removed from the country's major centers of population. Only the railroads covered the distance swiftly and comfortably, but not at prices that were within the budget of the average American family.

The horseless carriage, on the other hand, promised to "democratize" long-distance travel, to bring

Left: *In addition to promoting national parks in California, the Southern Pacific Railroad supported the creation of Oregon's Crater Lake National Park in 1902. The new park never enjoyed Yosemite's popularity, but its proximity to the railroad line attracted additional passengers during the summer. Courtesy of the California State Library, Sacramento.*

the national parks within the range of the middle class. It followed that both the political and economic bases of the reserves would be considerably strengthened. Mounting threats to the parks were made by proponents of irrigation and water-storage projects and further underscored the necessity of compromising some wilderness values to accommodate the automobile. Either preservationists conceded additional space for roads and parking lots, or they would have to learn to live with dams, power lines, aqueducts, and other forms of development even more destructive of the scenery.

Fortunately, with the revival of leisure travel following the end of World War I, the western railroads prospered once more. In fact, the Yosemite Valley Railroad alone averaged well over 20,000 park tickets annually between 1921 and 1925, making these the best years in its history.

Finally, though, with the completion in 1926 of the modern paved highway between Merced and El Portal, the automobile emerged victorious in the competition. Railway officials tried to counter this trend by reducing fares to their lowest level ever—only $10.50 for the round-trip —but to little avail. By

Right: *Although miles north of Yosemite, Lake Tahoe was a popular attraction often sold to travelers in conjunction with a trip to the national park. Courtesy of the California State Railroad Museum, Sacramento.*

LAKE TAHOE REGION

Southern Pacific

1928, the number of passengers on the Yosemite Valley Railroad had fallen almost eighty percent, and the next year, with the Great Depression close at hand, hope of making a significant recovery dimmed even further.

Having lost the bulk of its passenger business, the railroad relied on its equally sporadic freight operations. As a result, the line filed for bankruptcy in 1935; finally, in 1944, the owners of the Yosemite Valley Railroad petitioned the Interstate Commerce Commission for permission to abandon the route altogether.

Officials of the National Park Service, most notably Regional Director O. A. Tomlinson, protested the request. Terming approval of the abandonment "a step backward," he received strong support from Michael W. Straus, acting secretary of the interior, who also urged the Interstate Commerce Commission that "in my opinion, it is doubtful that the present or future public convenience and necessity would be served by the abandonment of the Yosemite Valley Railroad." To the contrary, he concluded, "the Yosemite Valley Railroad can perform a needed and

Left: This luxurious brochure cover, ca. 1920, depicts Cathedral Rocks mirrored in the Merced River of Yosemite Valley. The Indian woman and papoose in the foreground represent the Miwok-Paiute culture indigenous to the region. Courtesy of California State Library, Sacramento.

valuable service in taking care of visitors to Yosemite National Park."

Several factors, especially the long decline in passenger numbers, worked to undermine these arguments. In June 1945, the Interstate Commerce Commission granted the Yosemite Valley Railroad permission to shut down. Following its last scheduled run in late August, the line was put up for auction, sold, and quickly dismantled for scrap. By the close of 1946, the Yosemite Valley Railroad, once hailed as the "Grand Central of the West," was history.

Within a decade, the misgivings of those opposed to abandoning the Yosemite Valley Railroad had been vindicated. In the wake of its dismantlement, the National Park Service was left with no other option but to provide for the hoards of motorists who descended on Yosemite Valley throughout the 1950s and 1960s. Finally, with annual park visitation in excess of two million people, it was dramatically apparent that the automobile must be controlled in the valley once and for all.

The first attempt came in 1968 with discontinuance of the popular firefall (burning embers of bark pushed off Glacier Point), whose nightly displays attracted thousands of motorists to Stoneman Meadow

---

Right: *Courtesy of the National Park Service, Yosemite Collections.*

YOSEMITE VALLEY
and the BIG TREES

Glacier Point, 3,250 feet above the Valley.

Southern Pacific

beneath the 3,200-foot cliff. Correspondents described the crush of people and cars as reminiscent of a huge drive-in movie, complete with litter, blaring radios, and after-show traffic jam. Because the firefall was an artificial creation, the National Park Service decided it could be sacrificed without jeopardizing the Yosemite experience.

The next major improvement was inaugurated in 1970. Park officials closed the eastern third of the valley to all private cars and, in cooperation with the concessioner, instituted a system of free shuttle buses to carry visitors between the trailheads and popular points of interest. Once restricted to walking or using mass transit, most people gladly chose the latter alternative.

Subtle but unmistakable coercion brought much-needed improvements to Yosemite Valley. Vegetation returned to trampled meadows; for the first time in years, park visitors could walk beside the roadways or ride their bicycles without being intimidated by long strings of onrushing cars. Equally significant, the shuttles themselves became very popular once the public learned to appreciate both their convenience and their role in salvaging Yosemite Valley from the congestion of the automobile.

As a result of these efforts to remove intrusive automobile traffic from the park, during the initial preparation of the Yosemite General Management Plan in 1974 and 1975, the National Park Service asked the public to consider the restoration of the Yosemite Valley Railroad itself. Fully twenty-nine percent of all respondents to the planning questionnaire indicated that rebuilding the railway would be a desirable option. Some people argued, for example, that storage lots planned for cars just outside the valley would still intrude upon the national park ecosystem by merely transferring the congestion and pollution to the periphery of the reserve.

The proposal was not adopted; instead, the right-of-way of the Yosemite Valley Railroad was to be upgraded and maintained as a bicycle path in cooperation with the U.S. Forest Service. But persons fond of the Yosemite Valley Railroad have not lost hope for its restoration sometime in the future. The popularity of the shuttle system in Yosemite Valley is proof that many Americans are willing to make greater use of mass transit. Rebuilding the Yosemite Valley Railroad would combine optimum security with maximum visitation for the national park, regardless of the future of the American automobile.

The trip by rail up the Merced River Canyon on the way to Yosemite National Park was described by early travelers as one of the high points of their journey. Courtesy of the National Park Service, Yosemite Collections.

Mt. St. Helens from Spirit Lake

In the Glorious Pacific Northwest

A quiet lake, fir-fringed—mirroring a snowy mountain peak. Sunlight glistening on the crest of Mt. St. Helens, and sifting the mysterious shadows of the emerald forests at her feet.

This is but one of the sublime retreats in the Pacific Northwest—the ideal vacation land. I will be glad to send you illustrated booklets that will help you plan your trip.—A. B. S.

Mail this coupon to A. B. Smith, 838 Northern Pacific Building, St. Paul, Minnesota

Books or trips I am Interested in (√) — Round Trip Summer Fare from Chicago

☐ Yellowstone Park	$ 59.35
☐ Pacific Northwest { Portland	90.30
☐ Rainier Park { Seattle / Tacoma	90.30
☐ Alaska (Skagway)	190.30
☐ Rocky Mountains (Helena—Butte)	61.95

"Route of the North Coast Limited"

MY VACATION TRIP

Name

Address

Northern Pacific Railroad advertisement, 1926, reprinted by permission of Burlington Northern Inc.

76

EPILOGUE

Burlington Northern and the Legacy of Mount St. Helens

SEATTLE, May 18—Burlington Northern Inc. today announced it will donate a unique piece of property to the U.S. government—the summit of Mount St. Helens.

Burlington Northern Inc., 1982

THE AMERICAN PEOPLE, for all their love of Yellowstone, the Grand Canyon, Glacier, and Yosemite, have largely forgotten their debt to the railroads of the West for first bringing these and other national parks into the life of the nation. To many, the golden age of rail passenger service died on May 1, 1971, when the National Railroad Passenger Corporation, popularly known as Amtrak, took responsibility for the few surviving long-distance passenger trains in the United States. The railroads themselves, now largely indifferent to passenger service, made little protest as Amtrak sacrificed the unique color schemes, vista dome cars, and other marks of individuality that had made the original trains so distinctive in appearance and so enjoyable to ride.

Imagine the astonishment that must have greeted the announcement on May 18, 1982, that Burlington Northern Inc., intended to deed its property on the summit of Mount St. Helens in Washington state to the federal government. Two years earlier to the day, Mount St. Helens electrified the public as a magnificent geological spectacle. Only a few Americans, however, were aware of the historical significance of Burlington Northern's square mile of property on the crest of the mountain.

"The great American vacation," 1924 advertisement, reprinted by permission of Burlington Northern Inc.

The dedication of Mount St. Helens symbolized the western railroads' long and remarkable commitment to the establishment, protection, and development of the national parks. For nearly a century, beginning with the creation of Yellowstone National Park in 1872, the parent railroads of Burlington Northern Inc.—the Northern Pacific, the Great Northern, and the Chicago, Burlington & Quincy—opened the national parks of the Pacific Northwest to America and the world. The donation of the summit of Mount St. Helens was not exceptional for Burlington Northern Inc., but, more appropriately, it was a reaffirmation of its positive and colorful tradition of corporate philanthropy.

For many years, Mount St. Helens, like the historical legacy she would come to represent, slumbered in relative obscurity and isolation. Nationally, if not regionally, her fame and beauty were overshadowed by her renowned sisters to the north and south, Mount Rainier and Mount Hood, respectively.

Meanwhile, modern Americans had, for the most part, rejected the railroads as a viable source of travel; and gradually, the history and the significance of the railroads in opening the Pacific Northwest became only a dim recollection. Prior to the eruption of Mount St. Helens, few people realized that the peak fell within the boundaries of the federal land grant awarded in 1864 to the Northern Pacific Railroad to help offset the cost of its construction. Similarly, almost no one noticed in 1970 when the remainder of this grant, with the merger of the Northern Pacific into Burlington Northern Inc., became the property of the new corporation.

Then suddenly, early on Sunday morning, May 18, 1980, Mount St. Helens shook the Pacific Northwest with a thundering assertion that she, too, had a special place in the history of the region. The north face of the mountain blew apart, spewing smoke and ash tens of thousands of feet into the atmosphere. Simultaneously, millions of tons of mud, shattered tree trunks, and other debris swept down the northern slope, choking Spirit Lake and flooding the Toutle River.

The area devastated by the blast encompassed more than two hundred square miles, and sixty lives were lost among those persons closest to the mountain. No amount of training could have prepared the government agencies assigned to the disaster to cope with such a powerful and relentless force. It was weeks later, when no other major eruptions seemed imminent, before everyone began to appreciate the unique opportunity that now presented itself to chronicle the rebirth of the summit and its environs.

Burlington Northern Inc., as co-owner with the

Right: Northern Pacific Railroad advertisement, 1922, reprinted by permission of Burlington Northern Inc.

Mount St. Helens before, during, and after the eruption. Courtesy of the U.S. Geological Survey, David A. Johnston, Cascades Volcano Observatory, Vancouver, Washington.

federal government of Mount St. Helens, was especially concerned about the future of the peak, now a hollowed out, gaping crater 1,313 feet lower in elevation than the original. Extending from the lip of the crater down the slopes opposite the blast area, arcing ninety degrees from due south to due west, lay the remainder of the square mile that was part of the original grant awarded to the Northern Pacific Railroad. This portion of the mountain could form the nucleus of the park or interpretive zone proposed by preservation groups. As a result, Burlington Northern Inc., decided in 1982 to deed the entire section back to the federal government.

Richard M. Bressler, chairman and chief executive officer of the corporation, informed President Ronald Reagan by letter of the donation on May 17, 1982. "It is our hope," Bressler concluded, "that this donation will encourage the careful management of the Mount St. Helens area for the contemplation and enjoyment of future generations."

So, thanks to that eventful May 18th two years earlier, the stage was set for Burlington Northern to add another chapter to the history of railroad philanthropy on behalf of the American environment. A century ago, when the Northern Pacific Railroad planned its right-of-way across Washington state, no one could have foreseen that in 1982 the route would help to bring the Yellowstone legacy full circle. Mount St. Helens offers another geography of hope. Indeed, not since the discovery of the original national parks of the West has any landmark so captivated the American imagination, so reaffirmed the nation's pride in its breathtaking natural beauty.

On May 18, 1983, the third anniversary of the eruption, officials of the United States Forest Service, Burlington Northern Inc., environmental groups, and other interested parties convened for the dedication of the Mount St. Helens National Volcanic Monument and visitor center. Bressler presented a commemorative plaque on behalf of the Burlington Northern corporation, and further outlined the railroad's commitment to scenic preservation. Although the boundaries of the monument had not been laid out to the satisfaction of everyone concerned, no one disagreed that the protection of Mount St. Helens symbolized another positive step in the preservation of American land.

In a similar spirit of optimism, consumer advocates took heart in recent developments suggesting a renaissance for the passenger train. By 1983, Amtrak's eight major routes in the West had been completely reequipped with new coaches, lounges, diners, and sleeping cars, the first such renovation in the region in more than twenty years. During much of that year the trains ran at full capacity, proving conclusively that Americans had never totally forsaken the railroads.

In the 1960s, abandonment of rail passenger service in the West had been based on research suggesting that passenger trains could be profitable only when operated between pairs of major cities that were less than three hundred miles apart. By 1980, however, a new generation of railroad economists was predicting the resurgence of the long-distance passenger train as opposed to its short-haul competitor. Amtrak's trains between major cities in the Northeast Corridor had indeed carried a far greater number of commuters and business people; however, the commitment of these passengers was to the use of trains for only short distances. Thus, although the long-distance passenger trains carried only one-fifth of Amtrak's total ridership, they nonetheless accounted for over sixty percent of all passenger miles traveled and all ticket revenues collected by the company nationwide.

Such statistics demonstrated the importance of not only attracting a large number of passengers, but of carrying them far enough to offset the high fixed costs of buying and operating the equipment. Years earlier, Louis W. Hill, president of the Great Northern Railway, had reminded railroad executives that in promoting the national parks the key to profits was not only filling the trains, but keeping them filled for as long as possible. And for precisely this reason, Amtrak trains in the East had a much harder time covering costs, since most commuters and executives rode an average distance of barely one hundred miles.

In the West, however, the situation was quite the opposite. Not only did the average trip exceed one thousand miles, but Amtrak passengers in the region paid proportionally higher fares. The wide discrepancy in ticket sales could not be explained solely on the basis of the greater distances between western cities. Of equal importance was the fact that travelers in the West fully endorsed the once popular slogan "Getting there is half the fun," and, as proof of that conviction, they actually sought out the passenger train as a bridge to the western experience.

Public discussion regarding passenger trains dwelled less on the argument that they were old-fashioned and too slow, and more on their rediscovered advantages over the automobile, the bus, and the airplane for use in both business and pleasure travel. Airline passengers, squinting at the ground below, soon learned the truth of a slogan once popular among railroad ticket agents: "A man with his head in the clouds can't see the trees *or* the forest." Knowledgeable travelers welcomed the fact that railroad rights-of-way were free from the billboards, litter, and hamburger stands that cluttered the nation's highways. Finally, those whose concerns rested with safety and the environment took note that train travel was substantially safer, more fuel efficient, and resulted in less pollution than alternative forms of transportation.

These findings indicate that there is every reason

Amtrak's most popular "train of discovery," the Coast Starlight, runs parallel to the Pacific Ocean between Oxnard and Surf, California. Here the Starlight crosses Gaviota Trestle at Gaviota Beach State Park, northwest of Santa Barbara. Courtesy of the author.

to be optimistic about the future survival and prosperity of the long-distance passenger train. In addition, tourist railroads, whose patrons pay an extra premium for the unique experience of traveling on these special routes, have made substantial gains. Many train enthusiasts have applauded the announcement that restoration of rail passenger service to the South Rim of the Grand Canyon is pending. If this service from Williams, Arizona, lives up to its potential, then perhaps other such tourist railroads will call again at the gates of Yellowstone and Yosemite.

The heritage of discovery in America has been the subject of this book. Although nurtured in a naive, sentimental, and romantic age, the emotions that gave it life still have their place in contemporary society. Our respect for the reality of the West will not assure its survival; we must also preserve the region for what it means to American culture. There is reason, then, for hope that the trains, like the land, will survive — a bit less gloriously perhaps, but nonetheless alive with the excitement of millions of travelers who still answer the irresistable call of the national parks. May their joys of discovery, and their numbers, increase.

This Great Northern Railway express wagon displays the "See America First" slogan, a promotional tool designed to encourage national park tourism. Courtesy of Burlington Northern Inc.

A Note About the Sources

WITH THE EXCEPTION of my own articles mentioned in the acknowledgments, information about the western railroads and their role in developing the national park system is widely scattered. Primary sources include the annual reports of the superintendents of the individual national parks, published by the Government Printing Office, and Record Group 79 of the National Archives, the records of the National Park Service. The J. Horace McFarland Papers, housed in the William Penn Memorial Museum in Harrisburg, Pennsylvania, under the auspices of the Pennsylvania Museum and Historical Commission, also provide insightful glimpses into the attitudes of noted preservationists toward the western railroads just after the turn of the century.

For the role of the Northern Pacific Railroad in promoting the establishment of Yellowstone National Park, there are two recent works by Aubrey L. Haines: *The Yellowstone Story*, 2 vols. (Yellowstone National Park: Yellowstone Library and Museum Association in cooperation with Colorado Associated University Press, 1977) and *Yellowstone National Park: Its Exploration and Establishment* (Washington, D.C.: Government Printing Office and National Park Service, 1974). In both works, but mostly in the latter, Haines liberally reprints the pertinent documents which were issued by the offices of Jay Cooke and Company. *Nature's Yellowstone* (Albuquerque: University of New Mexico Press, 1974) by Richard A. Bartlett, and *National Parks: The American Experience* (Lincoln and London: University of Nebraska Press, 1979) by Alfred Runte are other scholarly interpretations of the events of 1869–1872, while Thurman Wilkins's *Thomas Moran: Artist of the Mountains* (Norman: University of Oklahoma Press, 1966) provides detailed summaries of Moran's relationship with Jay Cooke and A. B. Nettleton.

A stunning *Wonderland* series of guidebooks, published by the passenger department of the Northern Pacific Railroad between 1885 and the turn of the century, is provocative not only for its visual portrayal of the railroad's commitment to Yellowstone, but for numerous testimonials from travelers about their impressions of the park. Additional articles in the guidebooks cover such topics as agriculture, mining, cities, hunting, and wildlife conservation. *An American Crusade for Wildlife* (New York: Winchester Press and the Boone and Crockett Club, 1975) by James B. Trefethen, credits the Boone and Crockett Club for convincing the Northern Pacific to adopt its strong stance in defense of Yellowstone, especially as a wildlife preserve. The other side of the railroad's management personality, that which is reflected in the lopsided exchange of lands

leading to the creation of Mount Rainier National Park, is best summarized in John Ise's *Our National Park Policy: A Critical History* (Baltimore: Johns Hopkins University Press, 1961).

For the spread of national park promotion among the other western railroads, there are privately published guidebooks, pamphlets, and advertisements. *Sunset* magazine, the organ of the passenger department of the Southern Pacific Railroad at the turn of the century, is especially informative about the railroad's intense interest in the High Sierra parks of California. Similarly, *The Grand Canyon of Arizona* (Chicago: Santa Fe Railway, 1902) is a luxurious volume in the *Wonderland* series tradition, replete with pages of quotations from globe-trotters and dignitaries who visited the chasm. For John Muir's impressions about the Southern Pacific Railroad, there is *John Muir and His Legacy: The American Conservation Movement* (Boston and Toronto: Little, Brown and Company, 1981) by Stephen Fox.

Two contemporary publications describing Louis W. Hill and the Great Northern Railway's development of Glacier National Park are Mary Roberts Rinehart's *Collier's* series entitled: "Through Glacier National Park with Howard Eaton," parts I and II, *Collier's* 57 (April 22 and 29, 1916) and "The Son Who Showed His Father: The Story of How Jim Hill's Boy Put a Ladder to the Roof of His Country" by Rufus Steele, *Sunset* magazine 34 (March 1915). The proceedings of the national parks conferences of 1911, 1912, 1915, and 1917, published by the Government Printing Office for the U.S. Department of the Interior, coupled with the hearings on the National Park Service bill before the House Committee on the Public Lands, also demonstrate the depth of commitment among the western railroads to the national park system.

For a discussion of the relationship between the railroads and Stephen T. Mather during his tenure as director of the National Park Service, there are two excellent biographies: Robert Shankland's *Steve Mather of the National Parks* (New York: Alfred A. Knopf, 1970), now in its third edition, and Donald C. Swain's *Wilderness Defender: Horace M. Albright and Conservation* (Chicago: University of Chicago Press, 1970). Albright, Mather's assistant and the second director of the National Park Service between 1929 and 1933, recently left his personal papers to the University of California, Los Angeles, where they are currently being catalogued.

A detailed history of the Yosemite Valley Railroad can be found in Hank Johnston's *Railroads of the Yosemite Valley* (Long Beach, California: Johnston-Howe Publications, 1963); the museum of the National Park Service, Yosemite National Park, also contains records and photographs of the company.

Finally, the eruption of Mount St. Helens is graphically pictured and described in Rowe Findley's "St. Helens: Mountain With a Death Wish" *National Geographic* 159 (January 1981).

ALFRED RUNTE is assistant professor of history at the University of Washington, Seattle, where he teaches courses on the American West and American environmental history. A leading authority on railroads and conservation, he is the author of *National Parks: The American Experience* (1979), a social, cultural, and intellectual history of the national park idea. Since 1980, he has served as a seasonal ranger-naturalist in Yosemite National Park, California. Dr. Runte serves as an historical consultant to Burlington Northern Inc., and is on the board of directors of the National Association of Railroad Passengers in Washington, D.C. In addition to lecturing nationally on environmental and transportation issues, Dr. Runte has been a frequent contributor to numerous scholarly publications and major newspapers, including *The Conservationist, National Parks, The Journal of Forest History, Passenger Train Journal, The American West,* and *The Washington Post.*